The Wrath of Judge Lynch: Race Wars

JOHN ARNOLD HARGIS

CONTENTS

No tree takes so deep a root as prejudice.

(*American Proverb, Mid 20th Century*)

1 THE GREATHOUSE TRIAL

In December 1900, three black men were lynched by a mob, two in Rockport, Indiana, and one in Boonville, Indiana. This book examines the details of those hangings and the surrounding events and circumstances leading up to it. One such event, the criminal trial of a black man in Rockport in October 1900, provides noteworthy background to the three deaths at the hands of "Judge Lynch."

On Saturday, June 30, 1900, about six months before the hangings in Rockport and Boonville, Grandview Marshall James Lockard, was shot during an altercation with a young black man, Captain Greathouse. The town of Grandview, with a population of 775 citizens at that time, of which 108 were black, is located four miles up the Ohio River from Rockport.

It is not disputed that there was bad blood between the two men; however, the source of their mutual animosity is the subject of disagreement. According to the Rockport Democrat, Greathouse was a disorderly vagrant who had repeatedly defied Lockard's orders to move on, resulting in a clubbing of the allegedly recalcitrant Negro. Presenting a different perspective, the Rockport Journal reported that Greathouse was "a peaceable, industrious man but had been beaten severely by the police officer because he would not obey orders to get off the street...."

The description of the shooting was also in disparity. The Democrat related that there was a scuffle between the two men in which the Marshall failed to wrest the gun from Greathouse, who then held the weapon "in position" and fired into Lockard's chest. When the target fell to the ground, the shooter fired again at the Marshall, but the firearm misfired.

According to the contradictory account from the other paper, the young man had secured the gun in order to defend himself in light of past beatings at the hands of Lockard, and, in the physical encounter between the men, it went off resulting in the officer being shot. There was no mention of Greathouse aiming the firearm or of a second attempt to shoot the Marshall.

The bullet that struck the officer, age 55, passed through his left lung just below the shoulder, missing his heart. He was initially in critical condition but recovered. Immediately after the confrontation, Greathouse fled into the countryside. In the meantime, the Spencer County Sheriff, Dan Anderson, was summoned to search out Greathouse, who had procured from John Kennedy a horse that enabled the fugitive to reach the farm of John's father, Alex, a white farmer. Greathouse was permitted to hide out in the cellar of Kennedy's residence. Tracking him to the farm with the intention of conducting a search, the sheriff was initially informed that Greathouse was not there. Ultimately, the sheriff and his posse were allowed to investigate the premises and found the Negro in the cellar. Greathouse offered no resistance but begged the sheriff to protect him from mob violence. Although some talk of lynching was reported, when Anderson and his captive passed through Grandview, where throngs of people lined the streets, there was no attempt at violence. The Journal commended the citizens for their restraint.

According to the Spencer Circuit Court Order Book, Greathouse was charged on October 3, 1900, with attempted murder and disorderly conduct, and a bench warrant was issued for his arrest. He pled not guilty and waived arraignment. He was represented by W.C. Mason. Since there is no record of counsel being court appointed, the attorney apparently had been retained. Trial by jury was scheduled for October 20 but was postponed until October 26 in order to allow the taking of the depositions of two witnesses, Dora Davis and Willard Winters. Not counting the deponents, whose deposition testimony would be read into the record, there were 40 witnesses, including the Marshall, all of whom were ordered by the court to appear at the trial.

With the shooting having taken place on June 30 and the warrant having been issued on October 3, over three months later, Greathouse apparently was released after his initial arrest by Sheriff Anderson, an unusual result given the ultimate charge against him. Equally puzzling are the delay in filing the formal criminal allegations and the short time between the charge and the trial. Recorded history, unfortunately, does not tell us about the pressures facing the prosecuting attorney, the sheriff, and other players responsible for initiating the criminal case.[1]

At the trial, the following men were selected as jurors, with a listing by name, age, occupation, and race, "W" signifying white and "MU" signifying mulatto:

John Davis, 63, farmer, W

Joseph Adams, 35, servant, MU

J. E. May, 37, farmer, W

Alfred Kirk, 43, farmer, W

James Lindsey, 62, farmer, W

William Kokomoore, 63, farmer, W

Robert Lang, 50, farmer, W

George Hesson, 40, occupation not given, W

Basil Mosely, 50, carpenter, W

Albert Fletcher, 55, farmer, W

Fred Kokomoore, 58, farmer, W

John Mulzer, 40, occupation not given, W

---

[1] There is no census record for Captain Greathouse or for Eph Greathouse, as he was sometimes called; however, Dolpa Greathouse, a black male age 20, is listed as a resident of Grandview and a farm laborer, which, if he is one and the same, likely accounts for why Greathouse fled into the country and to Kennedy's farm, where he may have performed work alongside Kennedy's son John, age 21, who had provided him the horse.

The jury returned a verdict of not guilty, thus prompting Judge Swan to enter an order discharging the defendant from custody and setting him free. Several of the witnesses were white farmers, along with a grocer and a cooper. Also, among those testifying were Joe Holland, a black man and day laborer, and S.W. Stuteville, a white physician, the latter of whom may have furnished information on the injuries of one or both combatants. Other than Holland, none of those called to the stand were identified to be members of the black race.

The several months' delay by the prosecutor, surely under intense pressure from some of the rabblerousing citizenry, in charging Greathouse, may have derived from reservations of overcoming what must have been convincing evidence that the defendant acted in self-defense and was justified in his conduct. His injuries must have been severe for a black man to be spared judicial punishment for shooting a white policeman. Possibly, Greathouse's physical appearance following the clubbing may have influenced the prosecutor's decision not to rush the case.

Following the acquittal, ostensibly due to a brutal flogging, Marshall Lockard was potentially a target for being prosecuted for aggravated battery against Greathouse. No charge was ever filed against him.

It is quite likely that the finding of not guilty and the release of Greathouse without punishment gave the Rockport mob that hanged three black men the following December the validation it wanted for taking the law into their hands, spurious as it was.

E.M. Swan, later to serve as Judge of the Spencer and Warrick Circuit Courts, Rockport and Boonville, respectively, stands to the right of the presiding judge and in front of the window of the Spencer Circuit Court, Rockport, IN, circa 1898. Judge Swan presided over the jury trial of Captain Greathouse conducted on October 26, 1900, and the two grand jury proceedings of black men hanged in Rockport and Boonville in December, 1900.

Judge, Spencer Circuit Court

Spencer County Courthouse as it appeared in 1900. The Courthouse occupied the square block where the jail and hanging tree were located. The Courthouse burned in 1915.

2 WAYLAID AND MURDERED

Sometime between 1:00 and 2:00 a.m. on Sunday, December 16, Hollie T. Simons and his brother-in-law, Theodore Evans, both white, closed their barber shop located near the corner of Main and Third Streets in Rockport. When they reached Fifth and Main, the two parted, Simons setting off on foot towards his home about four blocks away on Elm Street, while Evans walked in the opposite direction to his residence on Walnut Street.

Simons, turning north from Main, traveled one block on Fifth Street, then, after passing the planning mill proceeded west on Elm where he lived with his wife and seventeen-month-old son. Though Rockport, a vital riverboat city at the time, had street lights on its main thoroughfares, side roads like Elm Street offered limited visibility.

Shortly thereafter, two Rockport residents, James Stateler and Frank Jones, returning home after being out for a Saturday night on the town, heard loud screams that seemed to emanate from somewhere near Coppage's Livery Stable on Elm. As they walked past the David Stillwell residence following the road Simons had taken, Stateler believed the screams were those of a drunk, but getting closer he changed his mind, saying it was a hog. Jones, for his part, insisted that the cries came from a dog under a nearby bridge. Close to where they had heard the screams, Stateler struck a match. In the light of the flickering flame, he saw the shape of a man. As he was trying to determine if the man was dead or alive, a wooden board hit the ground behind him.

"Some son-of-a-bitch throwed (sic) a plank at me," he yelled. (It was later determined that the thrown plank had been ripped from the side of a nearby wagon.) Turning around, he spotted a "colored fellow" approaching from the direction of Stillwell's.

What happened next is not clear. According to one newspaper report, Stateler said to the approaching stranger,

"We've got to do something for that man." The stranger agreed and, according to Stateler, all three men approached the fallen body. Stateler turned the man over so that blood could drain from his mouth.

The account of Stateler engaging the black man was noted in the December 21, 1900, edition of the Rockport Democrat, but there was no mention in its rival paper, the Rockport Journal, published on the same date, or in other numerous newspapers in Southern Indiana and Northern Kentucky. The only reference in the Coroner's Inquest is as follows: "That said party was first found lying in a pool of blood by Frank Jones and James Stateler, who gave the alarm, and while viewing the body unknown party (sic) threw plank at them."

Simons, age 29, lived on Elm Street between Fifth and Sixth Streets, so he must have been attacked only a short distance from his home. Several of his Elm Street neighbors, including Mrs. William Tucker, John Howk, David Stillwell, and Mrs. Hammond, in the formal investigation of the crime, said they had heard a commotion in the street outside their homes that morning. The closest resident to the fatal encounter, Mrs. Tucker, testified at the inquest that, from her window, she witnessed a scuffle and saw "two or three men" fighting.

Simons was carried to the home of his brother-in-law. Never regaining consciousness, he died at 4:20 that morning. He had suffered numerous wounds including at least twelve blows to the head and a crushed skull. Based on the nature of penetrations to his head, one of the weapons was determined to have been a spiked club. His overcoat pocket contained $44.80, equal to about $1,307.89 in today's money. A goodly sum of cash, if it was a robbery, it is likely the arrival of Stateler and Jones kept the murderer from getting the money.

Barber, Hollie Simons, who was slain near his home on Elm Street of Rockport in the early Sunday morning of December 16th, 1900.

Simons was carrying an umbrella and a dinner basket at the time of the attack. The iron handle of the umbrella was broken and twisted, suggesting that Simons fought his attacker. Tracks of sock feet were found on the sidewalk, the street gutter, and the stable lot near where Simons was discovered.

On the Tuesday following his death, Simons' body was taken by train to Winslow, Indiana, his former hometown. Accompanying the remains were A.J. Glackman, undertaker, J. G. Rimstidt, Auditor of Spencer County, S. H. Jennings, real estate and insurance agent, and C. F. Baker, reporter for the Rockport Journal. The Pike County Democrat, published December 21, 1900, reported the following:

> Business was practically suspended during the time of the funeral, which was attended by hundreds of people who had known Simons during his citizenship of Winslow and who respected him. At two o'clock the funeral services were conducted at the M. E. Church by Rev. E. M. Hale. The minister paid a high tribute to the deceased whom he had known many years, and which brought tears to the eyes of many in the large audience. After the services at the church the

funeral cortege moved to the Oak Hill cemetery where The Knights of Pythias[2] performed the last sad rite.

The Rockport Democrat expressed similar praise for Simons, who had lived in Rockport for about three years, stating that no young man was held in higher esteem and that he had a reputation for being strictly temperate, industrious, and upright. Given such high acclaim, it was no doubt out of character for him to be going home to his wife and infant son at between one and two o'clock on a Sunday morning.

A barbershop on 3rd Street across from the courthouse in Rockport, IN, circa early 1900s.

---

[2] The Knights of Pythias is a fraternal organization and secret society founded in Washington D.C. in 1864. Five years after its founding, a black lodge was denied a charter by the Knights of Pythias Supreme Lodge in Richmond, Virginia. Both organizations, independently, pursued philanthropic and charitable goals.

3. ARRESTED AND LYNCHED

As word of the barber's fate spread throughout the community on Sunday, the call came to enlist the skills of a bloodhound, obviously of wide repute, from Morganfield in Union County, Kentucky, approximately 100 miles southwest of Rockport. The two-year-old canine, named "Dick," owned by E. H. Taylor, soon arrived in the care of Union County officials, Sheriff A.W. Clements, and Jailer James W. Snodgrass, after being ferried across the Ohio from Owensboro, Kentucky, about seven miles downriver from Rockport. A carriage was waiting to rush them to the city with all possible speed.

By the time of the arrival of the Union County contingent at 5:00 p.m. that Sunday, Spencer County Sheriff Dan Anderson and Rockport Marshall Tom Ellis had already arrested and detained several black men, including Bud Rowland and Jim Henderson. Several citizens reported that the latter two were seen on Main Street late Saturday night and, according to the account in the Rockport Democrat, several other witnesses said the men were "in the attitude of hatching a scheme for some meanness" and acted like they were "watching for someone to come along." Their suspicious conduct was enough to merit their warrantless arrests.

Having arrived in Rockport, Dick was taken to the scene of the crime where he picked up a telltale scent from the sock prints near the spot where Simmons was found dying. Dick, his nose to the ground, proceeded about 150 yards north through a lot, only to retrace his steps, as if to make evident that the person being tracked had returned to determine if the intruders, Stateler and Jones, were still at the scene. The dog then turned back to his former path, following the scent to the back door of the home of Rowland's mother, six blocks away, and into the room where Rowland had slept that night. There, investigators found the blood-stained pants Rowland was wearing on Saturday. The bloodhound's track indicated Rowland left his mother's that night and went to the Fourth Street home of his girlfriend with whom he was living. The house, owned by a man named Johnson, was known as place of ill repute. Rowland's blood-splotched hat was found there, and, when his female friend was asked about the blood stains, she admitted trying to wipe the hat clean that morning. She, too, was arrested.

Several people had joined the bloodhound's search, and shouts were heard to "get a rope." The dog then led the throng, now several hundred in number, to the jail. Once there, Dick, with officers in tow, entered, climbed the stairs, and went to the cell where Rowland was incarcerated. When confronted with the condition of his hat and trousers, Rowland claimed that he had killed a chicken on Saturday for his sister, an explanation the authorities rejected out of hand.

DICK.

Dick the bloodhound from Union County, KY. Summonsed by the Rockport mob to track down the alleged killers of the barber, Hollie Simon.

By this time, it was estimated that as many as 1,000 to 1,200 citizens had gathered in the vicinity of the courthouse and jail, which occupied the same block on Main Street between Second and Third Streets, as well as in front of the Veranda Hotel located on Main Street across the street from the courthouse square. One of the first indications that the mob, none wearing masks or in any way trying to conceal their identity, meant business came when a volley of about 50 gun shots were released into the air in front of the hotel. Seeing the crowd's feverish state, Sheriff Dan Anderson entreated them not to resort to mob violence and to let the law take its course. but he soon realized they were too frenzied to listen to reason. Fearing innocent people might be killed and knowing there was no chance of spiriting the prisoners away, Anderson locked down the jail.

VERANDA HOTEL

Veranda Hotel, located across from the courthouse square in Rockport, IN, where the lynching of Bud Rowland and Jim Henderson took place.

At the very time the frenzy of the mob was reaching a heightened state, Prosecutor Phillip Zoercher, who had come from Tell City, and Coroner Harry Harter, along with a stenographer, were in the sheriff's office taking statements in the investigation of the barber's death. The gun shots from the throng were fired just below their window. At about 7:30 that evening, a lone shot pierced the air, followed by the cry: "Come on!" The side door leading to the hall between the sheriff's residence and the jail was broken in. Using a sledge hammer, the crowd tried to pummel the heavy iron doors to the jail's entrance, but the task proved too difficult. Access was again denied when the iron grated window on the west side of the building would not yield. Some of the mob then seized a telephone pole 20 feet long and twelve inches in diameter to use as a battering ram against the outside, west wall.

Their mission finally accomplished, the men rushed through the breach into the jail. Rowland's cell was the first stop. He was reported to have beseeched Henderson to give up, but Jim protested and said that he would fight to the bitter end. It was noted in The Rockport Journal that "Henderson's suspicious actions that night and his bad reputation were about the only evidence against him."

Rowland was dragged out through the makeshift entry hole to a howling outcry of triumph. With the noose secured around his neck and the other end dangling from an overhead tree limb, he was permitted to say his final words, bringing an eerie silence from the otherwise rowdy onlookers. "Jo and Jim gave me whisky and got me into it," was his supplication. He claimed that Henderson made him drink it at knife point. He went on to assert that "I held him [Simons] while they beat him. Get Jo." Rowland's desperate plea earned him no reprieve. He was hoisted up, then riddled with bullets.

Jo Rolla, a Negro, worked as a porter at the nearby Veranda Hotel. The dying declaration by Rowland fingering Rolla as the primary culprit in the murder was the first and only information casting suspicion on him.

With the fatal dispatch of Rowland, the mob returned to the jail to seize Henderson. As they dragged him through the corridor, he grabbed a steel bar that had earlier been loosened and attempted to resist his captors. In the words of the Rockport Democrat: "A clear shot rang out in the stillness of the jail and Jim was a good nigger from that time on." The newspaper went on to report Henderson's last words: "Get Hustling Jo."

Although already dead from the from multiple gunshot wounds, Henderson was dragged out before the frenzied throng where another noose waited to hoist his body alongside Rowland.

The incrimination of Jo Rolla by Rowland spurred part of the mob, filled with blood lust, toward the Veranda Hotel. There they were confronted by O. B. Debruler, the owner of the establishment. He and others at the hotel told the crowd that Rolla was working there at the time in question and so could not have participated in the murder of Simons. Nevertheless, the lynch mob was beyond reasoning and searched the hotel's basement but without success. Forbidden to go upstairs where lodgers were staying, the mob reluctantly left the hotel and abandoned the search for the night. Rolla had been concealed under a bed in the guest room of a traveling salesman.

Rowland and Henderson were left hanging until the next morning. Prior to being taken down by the coroner at about 8:00 a.m. Monday, souvenir seekers carried away pieces of rope and material from the men's trousers, as well as twigs and bark from the tree from which they dangled.

Most gruesome of the relic gathering was the severing of parts of fingers of the dead men, one of which was used as a swizzle stick to stir an alcoholic beverage toasted in celebration of the event. A few weeks later, an actual postcard depicting the two men hanging from the tree, along with unmasked men beneath them, was printed for mass mailing or for a keepsake.

The sheriff, hoping to find an opportunity to get Rolla out of town without being seen, kept him hidden at the Veranda. He had arranged for a fast team of horses kept in Feigel's stable located across the back alley behind the hotel. At noon, he decided that the escape route was clear and brought the prisoner down the back way of the hotel and across the back alley to a buggy with side curtains concealing its interior.

The Sheriff's plan was to transport Rolla to the jail in Boonville, where he would wait for the train to complete the trip to Evansville, about 30 miles west of Rockport. The plan was quickly discovered by some of the vigilantes who congregated at Sexton's Drugstore to plan their assault. Word was sent by telephone to various points on the route to Boonville in hopes of intercepting the sheriff and his passenger. Converging from all over, men arrived in ones, twos, and threes in pursuit.

The careful planning by the sheriff and his speedy steed enabled him to outrun the pursuers. Rolla was no sooner lodged in the Warrick County jail than Anderson learned of their coming. He wanted to get Rolla to Evansville, but a large contingent of Boonville citizens demanded that the prisoner remain there. Anderson decided that it was too risky to move Rolla in the face of an angry crowd.

At about three o'clock that afternoon, some of the lynch gang from Rockport arrived on the outskirts of Boonville. A few ventured into town in order to reconnoiter the situation and the surroundings of the jail to determine how to break into the jail and lynch Rolla. Soon joining them were about 200 citizens from Winslow, Simons' hometown, who had heard that Rolla was in Boonville. Also, not wanting to miss out on the fun were several men from Kentucky.

As soon as the shades of evening fell, the waiting marauders, armed with ropes and crowbars and carrying a telephone pole, intimating at least some of them were most likely from Rockport, marched into Boonville. Led by a large, powerful man with a sonorous voice, none wore masks or disguises. Men, women, and children of Boonville lined the streets as spectators. A small boy among them yelled: "There they come!"

At this time, the Warrick County sheriff, Ben Hudson, was away from the jail, leaving Deputy Sheriff Ray Cherry in charge. When the mob leader demanded the delivery of the Negro, Cherry replied that he had no keys and could not comply. "Well, we'll just have to get him," was the retort. The execution of this declaration took only about thirty minutes of bludgeoning with the utility pole for the exterior jail wall to yield. Someone from the waiting crowd was heard to yell: "They will get him now for the big man is in!" "Whistlin' Jo," the moniker given Rolla by his accuser, Rowland, earned a brief reprieve when the intruders were delayed because they had to saw through the heavy iron bars to the cell. The clanging of chisels and crowbars sent reverberations through the rooms and corridors of the jail and out to the closely waiting throng, which fully expected the mob to meet resistance with a volley of gunfire from jail officers. None came. In a vain effort to escape his impending fate, Rolla had torn his mattress and tried to conceal himself in the center of the bedding.

A block and a half from the jail stood the courthouse where Judge E. M. Swan, of Rockport, whose judicial district covered Spencer, Warrick, and Perry counties, was holding court on an unrelated case. The court bailiff was sent out among the crowd to locate witnesses who were involved in the court proceeding. (It was reported in the Boonville Weekly Inquirer that the judge, at one point, went out to intervene and tried to suppress the violence but to no avail.)

With the mob upon him, Jo's body was said to have been trembling like an "aspin (sic) leaf." Cowering in the corner, poorly concealed in the mattress, the fateful target was seized and taken out to the anxiously waiting spectators. The leader shouted not to shoot for fear that an innocent person would be hit.

A large sycamore tree stood in the northwest corner of the courthouse, across from the St. Charles Hotel. A slight man who was among the jail crashers "climbed like a nimble cat up to the first large limb which shone white under the bright star light." As the hangman's noose encircled Rolla's neck, the leader granted him last words. "Have mercy on me. I didn't do anything. I was building a fire at the Veranda Hotel for a drummer who was staying there." "You are a black liar," shouted one of the mob. "String him up," came from another. Several men grasped the dangling rope, but, upon the first pull, the knot slipped. It was soon readjusted, and Jo was hauled up. The rope's end was tied to the trunk of the sycamore, leaving him dangling but not dead. His body jerked and twitched for at least two minutes, while his life was agonizingly choked out of him. Rolla died at about 8:30 p.m.

One more directive was issued by the man with the big voice: "The body will hang here until noon tomorrow, when it can be cut down." With that, the crowd started to disperse.

About two hours before the lynch mob descended on Rolla, Deputy Cherry had telephoned law enforcement in Evansville asking for reinforcements, but his request was denied on the grounds that there was no authority to so comply. His effort to deputize Boonville citizens also met with refusal. In his defense, the officer made the following statement to the Rockport Journal: "Sheriff Anderson and I had the buggy in the street next to the jail this afternoon at four o'clock and we were going to take the prisoner to Evansville by the overland route. I went to the cell and unlocked the door when I heard footsteps in the hall. There were a large number of Boonville people crowded in the hall. 'You had better keep him here, he'll be safe, and we will see that he stays here all night,' they said. I told them that it was for the best that we take him to Evansville, but they said 'no' and after consulting with my father I turned the key in the cell door and let the prisoner remain. It is the fault of the Boonville people. I was asked for the keys, but would not give them up, and when the determined men went to work I could do nothing save they have their way. To resist them would mean the loss of human life dear to us all without saving that of the prisoner. If they succeed in getting through those patented locks they will have him, for he is there."

As Rolla's body dangled from the Sycamore limb, someone among the onlookers yelled: "Hurrah for Boonville," which was repeated in roaring unison three times from the crowd, followed by a like number of cheers for Rockport. The crowd of men, women, and children who witnessed the event was estimated to number 2,000. A unit of the National Guard in Evansville, Company E, had earlier been ordered by the Indiana governor to go to Boonville to protect Rolla. However, they arrived too late.

Following an inquest conducted at 1:00 a.m. the next day, the Warrick County Coroner found Rolla's death was at the hands of "unknown men," though, of course, almost everyone including authorities knew who the unmasked men were. His body lay in state the entire day following his hanging, allowing hundreds to pass by his resting place to view his remains. The coroner's formal investigation in Rockport came to the same conclusion, i.e., no member of the mob could be identified. In the words of the Boonville Inquirer, in its December 21 publication: "There are none so blind as those who will not see." (The sole qualifications for the office of coroner were that he be eligible to vote and be a resident of the county where elected for at least one year prior to the election.)

Although state authorities vowed to ferret out those responsible for the lynching, the Rockport rowdies were determined to challenge such efforts. Such defiance was illustrated on the Friday following the hangings when two newspaper reporters from Indianapolis and two traveling salesmen were mistaken for detectives sent by the Governor. The four were kept under close surveillance and, when they left Rockport, they were followed to Huntingburg by men acting in behalf of the "Good Citizens League" of Rockport and were warned in stern terms not to come back to Rockport.

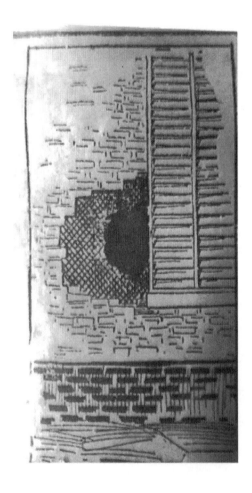

West wall of the Spencer County jail, with opening made by the mob using a utility pole.

Photo of Bud Rowland and Jim Henderson after being lynched by a mob in Rockport, IN, on December 16th, 1900. Postcards were mass produced from this macabre image, an undertaking that underscores the attitude of the time.

4 THE HANGED

Bud Rowland, whose name was variously given as Roland and Rollin, with first name possibly being Fred, was reported to have a bad reputation. He was 22 at the time of his death. His former residence was Cannelton, Indiana, a town about thirty miles east of Rockport on the Ohio River. He was blamed for bringing a smallpox epidemic to Rockport, which reportedly incurred $3,000 in medical expenses fighting the disease. He and Jo Rolla had been employed at Simons and Evans' barbershop as shoeshine boys but were dismissed for alleged misconduct. Rolla was from Edmondson, Arkansas, a suburb of Memphis, and was said to have come to Rockport as a fugitive from justice. He went by several nicknames, including Whistlin' Joe, Hustlin' Jo, and Crowfoot; his last name, according to different sources, may have been Rolley or Holley.

Jim Henderson, 28, had served time in the penitentiary for shooting another black man. During the weeks prior to the lynching, which Rockport people referred to as "the black fortnight," several stores and houses were broken into, including those of A.H. Kennedy (leading educator), T.C. Basey (druggist), E.D. Erhman (medical doctor), and John Wright (builder), all prominent, white citizens of the community. Although there was no evidence against him, Henderson was generally believed to be the head of the gang of Negroes committing the crimes and terrorizing the town.

The success of these marauders, whoever they were, and their ability to avoid detection, undoubtedly emboldened the mob. One can only speculate what influence the acquittal of Greathouse, only a few weeks earlier, may have had on their actions.

Rowland and Henderson were buried adjacent to one another in Block 3, Row 19, Plots 10 and 11, in the pauper section of the Sunset Hill Cemetery, located on the outskirts of Rockport. There are no grave markers commemorating their deaths. However, in the Rockport Cemetery Register, there is a handwritten note alongside their names: "The two that was hung, was shot."[3]

In Boonville, Rolla's body was prepared for burial at Trimble's undertaking establishment. He was buried at Potter's Field next to the county poor asylum. There is no record of the exact place of his interment.

----

[3] The two plots are immediately south of the marked grave of Mattie Belle Mahoney, also buried as a pauper in plot 12, who, along with her unborn child, was shot in 1898 a few miles outside of Rockport by Owensboro, Kentucky, law enforcement while she was in the company of Howard Clark, a gangster from Southern Illinois. A local Rockport resident, Max Dawson, took an interest in her story and purchased a gravestone to commemorate her death. The stone step, formerly at the edge of the courthouse lawn leading to the place of the hangings, will serve as a burial marker for Rowland and Henderson.

Grave sites, with no markers, of Bud Rowland and Jim Henderson, who were hanged in Rockport by a mob on December 16, 1900. They are buried in the pauper section of Rockport's Sunset Cemetery next to Mattie Belle Malone, also a pauper. A local resident recently honored her with a burial marker.

Stone step leading from Rockport's Main Street to the site of the hangings of Bud Rowland and Jim Henderson from a tree in the courthouse square on December 16, 1900. This step will be moved to the gravesite of the two men to serve as a burial monument with relevant information of their deaths.

5 ANATOMY OF THE CRIME

Evidence of guilt in the murder of Hollie Simons points to Bud Rowland, based on the work of Dick the bloodhound, Rowland's bloody clothes, and his confession.

With his keen sense of smell, Dick identified Rowland's scent from the sock prints, which led him to the bed Rowland had occupied at his mother's house. There the man's bloody trousers were found, followed by discovery of Rowland's blood-splotched hat at his lady friend's, again the work of the canine sniffer. The next stop for the dog was the very cell where Rowland was incarcerated.

In the face of the noose, Bud made a self-serving admission, shifting the blame, first to Henderson, who got him drunk "at knife point," then to Rolla, who "struck the first blow." Rowland painted himself as an unwilling accomplice.

As to Henderson's influence on Rowland, it was as if the latter was forced into a hurried state of inebriation at the scene of the crime, which renders the claim implausible. He must have been in some state of sobriety to be able to hold Simons down while the other two beat him to death, as Rowland claimed in an effort to lessen the degree of his culpability.

If Rowland were guilty of the murder, did he act alone? Only one set of footprints was found in the soil at the scene. Stateler, who, along with Jones, was the first to arrive at the scene, testified that "someone" threw a plank at him. That "someone" obviously meant to scare off the intruders in order to consummate the robbery. (In one account, Stateler said a lone black man appeared and agreed that the dying man needed help.) Neither Stateler nor Jones makes any mention of others being present. Mrs. Tucker, the curious neighbor who looked out the window at the sound of a scuffle, saw "two or three" men fighting, not four. If only two, it would have been the victim and another, presumably Simons and Rowland. If three, one of the accused was not present.

The fact that at least four residents on Elm Street heard a scuffle and that Simons' battered umbrella shows that he fought back raises the question whether he would have been capable of putting up a battle against three, or even two, attackers, particularly if they carried weapons, and that the brutal encounter produced enough clamor to attract several persons inside their homes.

If Henderson was one of the culprits, his scent was not picked up by the bloodhound, though he was in the cell next to Rowland when Dick sniffed his way to the jail. Plus, no blood was found on Henderson. His presence on Main Street earlier that night with Rowland may raise some suspicion, but no real evidence of complicity in the murder. In the jail, Henderson tried to fight off the approaching mob while at the same time professing his innocence. Unlike Rowland, he did not confess. Of course, Henderson could have been as culpable as Rowland, but there is just no proof to back that up. In any event, the lynch mob was blind to reason and bent on hanging both men. Hearing Rowland's confession, self-serving as it was, implicating Henderson, was, in their minds, proof enough for Judge Lynch. (A few newspaper accounts, without naming any source, reported that Henderson had confessed; mobs prefer confessions as a justification for their work and at that time in Indiana's history, many papers were happy to comply.)

Rolla was later exonerated, but that certainly did not help him. Several people, including his employer, vouched for Jo, and one anonymous person, after traveling to Indianapolis to see the Governor, offered to sign an affidavit to that effect. A wire story that was sent statewide, read as follows:

INNOCENT MAN LYNCHED

Indianapolis, Ind., Dec. 21.----Positive evidence has been secured by the state that the colored man, "Whistling Joe" Rolla, who was hanged by a Spencer county mob at Booneville (sic) Monday [December 17] night, was innocent of any participation in the murder of Barber Simon[s] at Rockport, and it is now questioned whether he even knew of the deed having been committed until the day after it happened....he died protesting his innocence almost his last words being: 'You are hanging an innocent man.' Subsequent investigations leave no doubts that he was at the hotel at the time Simon[s] was killed and had not been away during the night.

Several newspapers, including the Corydon Republican, reported the news of Rolla's innocence. However, the Rockport Democrat, published the same day, carried this sub-caption: "BUD ROLIN, JIM HENDERSON AND JO ROLLEY, TOUGH CHARACTERS PLACED UNDER ARREST. THEIR GUILT ESTABLISHED BEYOND ANY DOUBT." (Emphasis added.) Either the local paper did not receive the wire by the time of publication, ignored it, or disagreed with its finding. No retraction or correction was ever printed. In the same publication, the report of the lynching concluded as follows: "Not a single individual in the community has been heard to express regret at the work of the mob. Even the good colored citizens take a philosophical view and say, it is well as it is." Many mob sympathizers, and apparently, the Rockport Democrat, believed that Jo Rolla had confessed, and that belief served as justification in their minds for his hanging. Eye witnesses who were present when Rolla was dragged out and lynched vouched that he had protested his innocence to the end.

The standard of proof in a court of law, whether before a judge or jury, to achieve a finding of guilt in a criminal proceeding is proof beyond a reasonable doubt.

This stringent rule of law is based on the premise that it is better that 100 men go free than that one innocent man be falsely condemned. It is also in keeping with the principle that our justice system is governed by laws and not men. Only a jury harboring a mob mentality, such as was the collective mind of Judge Lynch, would have convicted Rolla.

Rowland was very likely complicit in murdering Hollie Simons. Henderson's complicity, based on the evidence, is unsure. As the editor of the Rockport Journal noted in coverage of the homicide, the only bases for the arrest of Henderson were the reports of his suspicious demeanor and his bad reputation, no doubt including as the alleged leader during "the black fortnight," when several white citizens were burglarized.

The horrible murder of the barber excited not only the citizenry but also law enforcement who quickly rounded up several Negros, including Henderson and Rowland, without court authorization. The general rule, established by the Fourth Amendment to the United States Constitution and applied to the States by the Fourteenth Amendment, is that, unless a law enforcement officer witnesses a criminal act, a court authorized warrant must be obtained applying the standard that there is probable cause, not mere suspicion, that the target of arrest committed a crime. Failure to do so may taint evidence later found pointing to guilt. Such omission by an officer of the law, in this case Sheriff Anderson, could well doom court convictions of both Henderson and Rowland. Likewise, the discovery of Rowland's bloody pants without a search warrant would in all likelihood have resulted in exclusion of that evidence in a judicial proceeding.

Like the mentality of the mob, law enforcement's convulsive want to achieve quick retribution would prove fatal to lawful prosecution. Rowland's confession could be used to prove his guilt so long as lawfully taken and not coerced. His bloody pants and hat provided the needed corroborative evidence, if lawfully obtained. Rowland's statement against Henderson, if obtained in a legitimate interrogation, fingering him as one of the murderers, would be excluded unless Rowland testified in court against Henderson, who, as a defendant charged with a crime, has the right to confront and cross-examine his accusers.

Incriminating information gathered from the bloodhound's tracking raises challenging legal issues. Such evidence was undoubtedly admitted as proof of guilt in trial court proceedings not reviewed by an appellate tribunal, which, unlike a trial court, can establish precedent to be followed by all lower courts. Such a standard, to be applied universally to all courts in the state of Indiana, was handed down as a matter of first impression by the Supreme Court of Indiana reviewing a criminal conviction in 1917.[4]

While recognizing the olfactory skills of bloodhounds, the Court reversed the decision of the lower court, which had admitted such evidence, and held that the conclusions of the bloodhound are generally too unreliable to be accepted in evidence in either civil or criminal cases. Such proof was considered too sensational and likely to be given too much weight by a jury.

----

[4] Ruse v. State, 186 Ind. 237, 115 N.E. 778 (1917).

6 FINGER-POINTING

The Boonville Weekly Inquirer reported that, on December 17, the date of Rolla's hanging, Judge E. M. Swan, present in Boonville that day, tried to disperse the vigilantes and urged them to let justice take its course. A few days later, the Chicago Record and the Pike County Democrat also reported that Judge Swan had tried to quell the violent horde. Having received this account, Indiana Attorney General Taylor, from his office in the state capitol, Indianapolis, criticized Swan and chastised him for witnessing the lynching and for knowing some who took part. In a subsequent issue of the Inquirer, Judge Swan stated that he was not present at either lynching, was not a member of the mob, and had no curiosity to see it.

Swan was elected in 1898 as the sole circuit court judge serving three counties. He ran on the Democrat ticket and defeated his Republican challenger, Thomas E. Snyder, by 77 votes. If the judge did, in fact, confront the mob in Boonville, which was spearheaded by the contingent from the judge's hometown, he would likely have seen some of his supporters. Republicans, during that time, were adherents of anti-slavery and the party of Lincoln, the Great Emancipator, whereas the Democrat party sympathized with the South and the institution of slavery. There was no further investigation of the role of Judge Swan, which was not unusual for that time.

At about 6:00 p.m. on Sunday, December 16, before Rowland and Henderson were shot and then strung up, Spencer County Sheriff Daniel Anderson, a Republican who had won his election in 1898 by a margin of 302 votes, spoke to Indiana Governor James Mount to inform him of the dire situation and that the mob was battering down the jail doors. The Governor ordered a company of the Indiana Militia to move from Evansville to Rockport, but the movement was canceled when word of the men's fate was received before the troops' departure.

A similar scenario played out in Boonville the next night with the militia arriving only to see Rolla dangling from the sycamore. Holding Sheriff Anderson to blame for the lynching of Rolla, Governor Mount issued the following statement: "If he had not been derelict in his duty, this second lynching would not have happened."

Facing frenzied throngs bent on exacting vengeance in two different towns, Sheriff Anderson was up against difficult odds. It was reported in several out-of-state newspapers, including the Washington, D.C. Times, that the sheriff and his deputies made a stand against the mob in Rockport but were disarmed, locked in a room, and placed under guard. The sheriff refused to give up the keys to the prisoners' cells or to reveal where they were locked up.

In his treatment of Jo Rolla while still in Rockport, Anderson could have put him in a jail cell, only to have a repeat hanging at the hands of the mob. Instead, he kept the prisoner concealed in the Veranda Hotel, undoubtedly influenced by the owner's plea that Rolla was innocent. Finding an opportune time to make a clandestine escape to Boonville in a covered buggy, with the further intention to get Rolla to Evansville, a much larger city with more law enforcement, the vigilantes once again foiled his plan. The sheriff had arranged for a train to take Whistlin' Jo to Evansville once they arrived in Boonville, but the mob sympathizers in Boonville thwarted that move.

To Anderson's discredit, previous to the vigilante hangings in Rockport and Boonville, sheriffs in Grant County in 1885 and in Boone County in 1894 had confronted and dispersed mobs with a show of force.

Ironically, in 1892, just six years before his election to Indiana's highest office, Governor Mount had been the leader and president of the State Horse Thief Detective Agency. This organization, a vigilante group that operated outside of the law, caught and imposed punishment (even lynching) of livestock thieves, bypassing the judicial system and disregarding due process. When he took office, he weakened the policy of his predecessors to suppress such lawless enterprises, including the White Caps which operated unimpeded in Crawford and Harrison Counties in Southern Indiana. (By some accounts, Mount had been a member of the White Caps before his election to the governorship.) To his credit, he was not a racist. During the Spanish- American War, Mount tried to convince the United States War Department to engage Indiana's regiments of black troops, which had been first organized to fight in the Civil War. When the Department refused to accept them unless commanded by white officers, Mount appealed to President William McKinley who overruled the War Department, thus making the initial steps towards racial equality and integration of the United States Army. As further proof, White Cappers lynched just as many whites as blacks.

Although Governor Mount reluctantly supported anti-lynching legislation passed by the Indiana Legislature in 1889, he failed to aggressively enforce its provisions. The new law provided for a sheriff to forfeit his office in the event of failure to quell the lynching of a prisoner. In addition, it required that the governor be notified by the sheriff of mob activity with a view toward ordering the Indiana Militia to the scene. The mob violence in Rockport provided Governor Mount with his first opportunity to enforce the new anti-lynching law. Although Mount, a Republican, vowed to take action against Spencer County Sheriff Anderson, also a Republican, the matter was quietly dropped. Again, while Mount was still in office, following the hanging of a jailed black man from a bridge over the Wabash River near Terre Haute in 1901, the county sheriff escaped any disciplinary action or loss of position. During and just before Mount's time as governor, it was estimated that at least 68 victims, both black and white, were stung up as the result of vigilante justice, mostly in the southern part of the state. No law enforcement officers lost their jobs or received punishment.

Enforcement of the anti-lynching law changed dramatically under the administration of Mount's successor, Winfield Durbin, who took office in 1901. Beginning in 1902, numerous officials who failed to uphold the 1899 law were removed from office. In Sullivan County, where a mob forced the sheriff to surrender a jailed black man, soon to be lynched, Governor Durbin summarily removed the sheriff from office. Some of the mob participants, close friends of the sheriff, defended him, claiming that they would accept death at the sheriff's hand rather than have their wives dishonored by "negro fiends." The sheriff implored that he could not shoot his friends. The Governor, unmoved by such supplications, carried out the removal.

7 GRAND JURY

On March 24, 1899, over a year before the tragedy in Rockport and Boonville, the Rockport Journal, John Chewning, Editor, carried the following article addressing Indiana's new anti-lynching law passed in 1899:

Anti-Lynching Law

Under the new law it will not be comfortable to be even a passing spectator at a lynching bee. This constitutes a crime. Death or life sentences will be given to those who engage in lynching, and it is a felony to conceal or aid lynchers. Sheriffs or other officers are liable to impeachment for allowing a prisoner in their custody to be lynched. Bystanders may be armed to aid him and they dare not refuse such assistance on penalty of imprisonment from one to two years. It is thought that this will be an effective remedy against mobs.

It goes without saying that, for a law to be effective, it requires compliance by those who are governed by its terms, which was totally lacking on December 16 and 17, 1900, in Rockport and Boonville, Indiana. That same defiance of the law occurred during two grand jury proceedings ordered to be convened by Judge Swan.

On December 26, the Warrick County grand jury was chosen and met in special session to investigate Rolla's hanging. Members of the jury were Homer A. Gordner, John Trisler, Jacob Fisher, John Hodges, Jacob Tuley, and Elijah Philips. Because several prominent persons were known to have been members of the mob, the general consensus in Boonville was that no indictments would be returned. Even the Warrick County Prosecutor, Thomas Lindsey, who had been elected on the Democrat ticket in 1898, echoed the sentiment of the citizenry. In a statement to the Evansville Courier made two days following Rolla's lynching, Lindsey, Warrick County's top law enforcement officer, declared:

> I am of the opinion there will be no indictments returned. There were some of the leading citizens in the county in the mob, and the general opinion is they did a good job when they hung (sic) Rolla. While we do not endorse mob law, we

certainly believe criminals should be punished. The lynching of Rolla and the other two negroes at Rockport have done much to raise the standard of the law in the eyes of those who desire to break it. Suppose Rolla had been taken back to Rockport and tried for the murder of H. L. Simons. It would have been impossible to convict him.

There is no record of Prosecutor Lindsey's position when it was later determined that Rolla was innocent. A similar sentiment was expressed concerning the Rockport hangings by a United States Marshall who stated that he was not surprised at the work of the mob in view of the fact that Negroes there had become "overbearing and lawless."

Although grand juries, independently, have the power to call and even subpoena witnesses, for all practical purposes, the prosecuting attorney controls the proceedings and dictates who will testify. As is customary, the circuit court judge appears before the tribunal only initially (and not during the proceedings) to instruct the jurors on the law and, in the case of a specially called grand jury, to inform them of the matter they are to investigate, as Judge Swan did in a brief appearance in Boonville. The courtroom was packed at the time of the judge's arrival, with some spectators hanging from windows. Once the jurors had received their marching orders, the crowd was dispersed to allow them and the prosecutor to meet in private.

In Rockport, prior to the commencement of the grand jurors' investigative undertaking in the regular January term, Judge Swan informed them in detail of the statutory laws pertaining to lynching that are summarized in the excerpt from the Rockport Journal printed at the beginning of this chapter. He followed his instructions to the jurors with this statement:

> It is only a reiteration of what everyone knows to say that mobs are unlawful, and that those who participate in their work are themselves violators of the law. It is sometimes urged as an excuse that courts and juries do not do their duties. I am glad to know that with very rare exceptions such criticisms are entirely unfounded, and that those who indulge in them speak intemperately, without knowing the evidence or want of evidence in a cause, or the circumstances upon which the courts and juries are called to act.

> The law and its administration are the outgrowth of the wisdom of all past ages, and sometimes when its administration seems to miscarry, it is not so much the fault of those trying to administer it, as of the formalities of the law itself, or its

infirmities, or the lack of proper evidence to meet the requirements of the law itself.

Courts and juries, it is true, are only human and finite and fallible, and no doubt sometimes make mistakes. And who does not? But almost without exception, I feel safe in saying, they do discharge their duties according to the best light they have at the time. And although it may be unnecessary, it is proper that I should mention to you at this time that a lax administration of the law by courts and juries is charged at times as an excuse for mob law, should urge them to always endeavor to ward off such reproach, as well as protect society, and discharge their duty, by a proper effort to administer the law at all times and under all circumstances under the law as prescribed to them, and under the evidence as furnished to them, and under sanction of their consciences, that best of all monitors.

But whatever imperfections may be found in the laws and courts, they are ultimately the best safeguard of our lives, our liberties and our rights---and against the rule of anarchy. Mob rule is not only unlawful, but it is dangerous in its tendencies, and may be frightful in its consequences, and the authorities should use all proper means in their reach to prevent and frustrate mobs and teach them proper respect of the law.

(It is worth noting parenthetically that Judge Swan's declaration that the miscarriage of justice in the judicial system "is not so much the fault of those trying to administer it" is precisely what occurred in Rockport by those officials charged with such responsibility, i.e., the prosecutor, sheriff and other law enforcement, coroner, and judge, who failed to seek indictments of known participants.)

The grand jurors in Rockport were Willis Haines, Thomas Markland, John Bauer, Charles Schumacher, James Crews, and James Ensor and were sworn to follow the instructions of the court and the law by the Clerk of the Court, John Baumgaertner. Each agreed to do so on his separate oath, "so help me God."

No indictments were returned either by the grand jury in Rockport or by the grand jury in Boonville. Because such proceedings are secretive, no witnesses who testified before the tribunals were identified. It was reported that the grand juries made a "careful" investigation of the mobs' work, and, as expected, not a single member of the mob in either city could be identified. No persons were determined to have aided the mob, and no law enforcement officers were found to have failed in their duty to uphold the law. (It was reported that a young man named Walter Evans, after witnessing the lynching of Rowland and Henderson, suffered a nervous collapse and became a "raving maniac." Evans was the only person identified to have seen the hangings.)

With photographs of members of the mob, standing proudly next to the hanged men, it is self-evident that the coroner, the sheriff, the prosecutor, judge, and the grand jurors were in approval of the lynchings in Rockport, as well as in Boonville, or, at least where applicable, fearful of their chances of retaining their offices in the next election. The Rockport hangings were later depicted on a postcard, ostensibly for mass mailing or as a keepsake, with the plain-faced executioners standing proudly just below the two dangling men.

The decisions of the grand juries served, to some extent, as an unbefitting vindication for Sheriff Anderson who could say that none of the mob could be identified, leaving him helpless to impose order. He later made the statement that the lynching would have the effect of stopping lawlessness on the part of Negroes in Rockport.

The refusal of grand juries to name mob participants, even though well known, was undoubtedly the norm. In Scottsburg, Indiana, two years earlier, on Christmas Eve, a black man, Marion Tyler, was lynched by a mob for shooting his wife. A reporter from the Indianapolis Journal interviewed several of the community's citizens, who knew prominent people in the mob but refused to name them. Tyler's wife, who survived, admitted that she was glad to be rid of him, whether at the end of a rope or otherwise, and wanted no one prosecuted.

In a touch of irony, less than two months after the Spencer County grand jury failed to return one indictment arising out of the mob violence, 119 Negroes, along with two white men, were indicted by the grand jury in the February, 1901 term for selling their votes in the previous November election. Many of those charged fled the county. These indictments were an offshoot of the crusade to stamp out lawlessness following the lynching of Rowland, Henderson, and Rolla and focused on cleaning up corrupt politics and eradicating floaters who sold their vote to the highest bidder. In essence, it served to disenfranchise the black vote.

The vote buying process followed the same pattern each election. Representatives of the respective political parties, invariably white lackeys of those in power, would haul to the polls black males willing to sell their votes for a meager sum or a half pint of whisky, not to be delivered until the vote was cast. Each person to be paid off, regardless of whether he was literate or not, was instructed to ask the polling officials to assist him in marking his ballot. Once out of the voting booth, a signal would be relayed to the waiting political puppet that the vote was entered as instructed and to hand out the election payoff.

Negroes who were out of work and prone to vagrancy were easy prey to this scheme, orchestrated by whites in political authority. Yet, in the frenzy to wipe out crime, it was the blacks who were indicted. Apparently, it was difficult to identify those who engineered the election connivance.

8 ROCKPORT

At the time of Simons's death, Rockport was a prosperous and thriving community, owing much of its success to its location on the Ohio River where commerce flowed on packet and excursion boats. The city, with a population of 2,808 citizens, of whom 404 were Negroes, including mulattos, offered five hotels, seven grocery stores, two banks, five saloons, three barber shops, a college, and several livery stables. Industries included an ice factory, a stirrup manufacturer, a carriage and wagon manufacturer, a vinegar factory, two brewing companies, a foundry and machine shop, a chair factory, a brickyard and tile works, a lumber yard and planning mill, a steam laundry, a paper factory, and a button factory.

With few exceptions, blacks filled the occupations of laborer, servant, or housekeeper.

One of the most labor intensive industries and places of employment of a large number of blacks was the Pearl Button Company, located on the corner of Seventh and Vine Streets on the north side of town. Mussels were harvested from the river and served as the material for the buttons. From each half shell, as many as four round buttons were cut, and smaller holes were made in each for the insertion of thread. Each button had to be sanded and polished by hand.

The portion of the buttons not transported by land was carried on river boats after being moved by land over Old Plank Road to Rockport's Upper Landing.

Barge transporting mussel shells harvested from the Ohio River, destined for Rockport's button factory.

Another labor-intensive industry providing employment for many black citizens was the Underhill & Sons Brickyard and Tile Works. Work there was physically demanding. Many Negroes toiled in the hot kilns. Others shoveled by hand the clay that was used as the material for the bricks and tile. Wages were meager, and laborers were often beholden to their employer for debt they incurred.

Except for a small, impoverished outpost about one mile south of Rockport, called Little Africa, the Negro community was concentrated in the southwest portion of town. A few black women, mistresses of prominent white men, were provided residences separate from the members of their race. A majority of adult black women worked as housekeepers. At the time of the hangings, 72 mulatto children were the offspring of Negro domestic servants.

Rockport paper factory, sometimes referred to as the "Strawboard," a place of employment for both white and black citizens from the community.

Rockport's lower landing between the bluff and the Ohio River

Rockport brickyard where many blacks were employed to work
in the hot kilns

9 RACE WARS

In the southern counties of Indiana, where the dominant attitude was neither proslavery nor antislavery but more anti-Negro, some of the seeds of coming race wars were sewn following the end of the Civil War when incoming Negroes competed for farm jobs. Strong feelings grew against blacks, as well as those who hired them. Not only were they driven off, but sympathetic farmers had their barns burned and their machinery vandalized. Notices were posted on fences warning these employers against further hiring of colored labor.

In May 1865, a group of citizens from Warrick County adopted a resolution urging the prosecution of anyone who would "bring, harbor, or employ any negro or mulatto" into that jurisdiction, with the pledge to pay from their pockets "according to what we are severally worth" the cost of a competent counsel. A month earlier, the New Albany Ledger warned Negroes to stay in Kentucky and not come to Indiana, where jobs were scarce, including a statement of the disposition of the community "where almost the entire population, without regard to political sentiment, entertain[s] feelings of strong prejudice against them." In Evansville, in August 1865, two Negroes who were accused of robbing and assaulting a white woman were dragged from the jail and lynched, with their bodies left hanging from lamp posts; the incident precipitated a widespread riot against the colored population of the city.

As a result of such suppression, many blacks lost work and were forced into poverty in small town and cities. The blame for the commission of property crimes, such as burglary and theft, automatically fell on Negroes.

Following the hangings in Rockport and Boonville, blacks were ordered to move en masse out of numerous counties along or near the river, among them Perry, Pike, Warrick, Crawford, Harrison, and Dubois. Committees were formed in the various towns to carry out these extirpations. In Crawford County, only one Negro, Arch Alton, also known as "Uncle Arch," who was blind and deaf, was left alone; the remainder were forced to leave. In both Harrison and Crawford counties, the exclusion was strictly enforced.

In one instance, a young man challenged being run out when he opened a barber shop in Leavenworth, a river town in Crawford County. He was a mulatto and considered by many to be trustworthy and industrious, resulting in some white inhabitants patronizing his business. When he repeatedly resisted efforts to run him out of town, his shop was broken into, and his equipment was thrown into the river. The vigilante horde tied the man to a skiff, and he was turned adrift in the midstream of the mighty Ohio, where he was left to the mercy of the current. Nothing was ever heard from him, and his fate was unknown. Similarly, in the Spencer County town of Enterprise, a Negro woman was fatally shot by her black husband by the name of Whitehouse, and he, along with the remaining Negro population, met the same fate as the Leavenworth barber when they were crowded into small boats and shoved out to meet the vagaries of the Ohio River.

In Rockport, immediately following the hangings, prominent citizens formed the "Good Citizens League" with the mission of imposing morality, stamping out gambling, establishing and enforcing curfews, and ridding the community of Negroes. Another target was vote buying, a practice followed by both political parties, with a disproportionate concentration on delivering the black electorate.

The 1910 census records show that the eradication of the Negro element in Rockport did not quite meet the success of counties like Crawford and Harrison. In the decade following 1900, the black population of Rockport dropped from 404 to 166, of which over one-third were mulattoes. Housekeepers and domestic servants with mulatto offspring comprised a large contingent of those spared being ostracized.

When it came to ridding communities of the unsavory, Crawford and Harrison Counties had a head start through the work of secret terrorist bands called the White Caps. Known for their white muslin hoods hiding the identities of its members, the group operated outside the law. Its mission was to enforce morality and to punish those who engaged in unrighteous conduct, regardless of their gender, age, or race. Even women and children were targeted. Wrongdoers, depending on the severity of their sinfulness, were whipped, flogged, driven off, even hanged. Transgressions included adultery, drunkenness, vagrancy, rape, family dereliction, theft, and murder. Many prominent persons, even law enforcement officers, joined in the vigilante enterprise. During its existence from 1880 to 1903, no White Cap was convicted of a crime. They acted with impunity while the justice system looked the other way. The White Caps was not a forerunner to the Ku Klux Klan which terrorized blacks and Republicans sympathetic with the anti-slavery elements and which did not formally organize in Indiana until over a decade after the demise of the White Caps. On the other hand, in 1926, there were as many as 300 active companies in the National Horse Thief Detective Association that formed alliances with the KKK. To a large extent, vigilante conduct was a carryover from the pioneer way of life when people fended for themselves without the assistance of government, which suffered from the reluctance of the citizenry to adequately fund public services, including law enforcement.

On December 24, 1900, just a week after the mob violence in Rockport, two black men, Lee Ranger and John Redmond, both intoxicated and armed, led a group that commandeered Sam Kendall's saloon in Cementville, near Jeffersonville, Indiana. Their next target was Kendall's nearby dry goods store where his wife was working. Kendall went to defend the frightened spouse and shot Ranger, whose companions carried him off. Being threatened by the Negroes, Kendall and his wife fled to Jeffersonville where he convinced Prosecutor Montgomery to obtain arrest warrants. Just a few days earlier, Jeffersonville police, in order to quell drunkenness and rowdy behavior, raided a black gambling facility, the "Warm Members' Club," and arrested several black men, including Ranger and Redmond.

Alcohol often served as a catalyst for violence, whether at the hands of blacks or whites. On Saturday night, December 15, 1900, at Curryville, a mining town near Sullivan, Indiana, several drunken coal miners tortured a runaway Negro boy. Being on his own without adult protection, the young man fell into the hands of the hell-bent miners. They branded his hands, face, and other parts of his body with a hot poker. He was then subjected to a mock trial to determine his ultimate sentence, with the proposed punishments being hanged, cooked in a red-hot stove, or thrown down a coal shaft. When cooler heads finally prevailed, his life was spared, and he was placed in the hands of the Sullivan County Sheriff. No one among the miners was prosecuted.

In 1903, one of the worst racial disorders in the history of the state was precipitated in Evansville, IN, when a Negro fatally shot a white policeman on the Fourth of July. Word of the killing soon spread, and a large contingent of angry citizens bent on lynching the shooter gathered outside the jail. Once it was learned that the prisoner had been taken to the jail in Vincennes, the mob went into various parts of the city to go "nigger hunting," meaning that if a colored man was sighted, he was fired upon. That day, clashes between the races became widespread and frequent. At the request of the Vanderburgh County Sheriff, Governor Winfield Durbin dispatched an entire company of the state militia to restore peace, which only fueled the antagonism of the crowd. When one of the mob pelted a guard with a large rock, gunfire ensued from both sides. Eleven members of the antagonists were killed and nearly fifty were wounded. Five guardsmen were shot by the mob but none fatally. Governor Durbin later declared: "Ostensibly [the mob was] seeking to avenge the murder of a policeman by a Negro, but actually engaged only in a senseless uprising against duly constituted authority."

Rather than face physical removal, many blacks in river towns fled in a mass exodus. Some crossed the Ohio to

Kentucky; others escaped north through Indiana to Quaker communities which sympathized with blacks.

Unlike the Quakers, a majority of the population in Indiana, and particularly the southern portion, considered Negroes to be innately inferior. Many held the view that God had made their skin darker as evidence that He intended them to be lesser in quality to fairer skinned people; moreover, the prevailing feeling maintained that the Almighty had placed blacks under a ban of Heaven rendering their cursed race unable to co-exist in peace with whites. Even a black author, William Hannibal Thomas, "frankly conceded the inferiority of his race."

With blacks being run out or leaving out of fear, it became a common practice for communities to adopt what became known as Sundown Laws. The Chattanooga Daily Times, on January 29, 1901, described the movement as an "Anti-Negro Crusade" and attributed it to mob justice in Rockport and Boonville, with this report:

> Cities and towns along the Ohio River have begun a crusade against the Negroes. The entire trouble dates to the lynching of Negroes at Rockport and Boonville for the murder of a white barber, Simons, at Rockport last month.

The Sundown Laws prohibited any black person from being within the city or town limits from sundown to sunup. As was the case in towns such as Cannelton, Tell City, and Troy, warning signs were posted at strategic points with this directive: "Nigger Don't Let The Sun Go Down On You In This Town."

Following the hangings of Rowland, Henderson, and Rolla on December 16 and 17, communities that adopted ordinances establishing Sundown status along or near the river, along with Cannelton, Tell City, and Troy, included Clarksville, Corydon, English, Ferdinand, Grandview, Chrisney, Huntingburg, Jasper, Leavenworth, Marengo, New Harmony, Newburgh, Petersburg, Vevay, and Winslow.

At the turn of the 20th Century, in Vevay, Indiana, the county seat of Switzerland County on the Ohio River, blacks in general were held accountable for murdering a white man named Hine. Negroes there were either hunted down and murdered or driven out. Vevay's Sundown Law remained on the books until the beginning of the Truman administration.

The New York Times, on June 17, 1902, published an article entitled "Bitter Race War Threatened French Lick and West Baden," two nationally known resort towns with prominent hotels noted for their healing spring waters, located a little over an hour north of Rockport. Sundown notices, adorned with skull and crossbones decorations, were placed in conspicuous places in the communities, as well as on the grounds of the hotels. At the time, the two health resorts relied heavily on colored labor, many of whom lived in a segregated hotel called "The Waddy." The reliance on Negro workers by the two high end establishments, which attracted celebrities and both famous and infamous national figures, may account for the only partial success of forced removal of blacks from the two communities.

The Sundown Laws were by no means limited to the southern part of Indiana. Numerous counties, cities, and towns in the central and northern portions of the state passed such laws, in keeping with Indiana being predominantly anti-Negro while at the same time against slavery. Decatur, located in the northwest corner of the state, is one such community notable in that regard. In another New York Times report on July 14, 1902, entitled "Negro Driven Away. The Last One Leaves Decatur, Ind.," it was reported that an Anti-Negro Society was organized, and a mob of 50 men drove out all blacks who had made Decatur their home, all due to what the Indianapolis Freeman newspaper reported on June 14, 1902 as "Negrophobia."

Indiana's Sundown Laws were, in a sense, the counterpart of the Jim Crow laws (a term derived from a minstrel song called "Jump Jim Crow"), passed in the South following the Reconstruction period, designed to keep the colored man in his place and segregated from whites. Pursuant to these enactments, facilities and amenities provided to white people were either denied to blacks or furnished in an inferior manner. Indiana enacted seven Jim Crow laws in the areas of miscegenation and education between 1869 and 1952, the last one invalidating marriages between the races.

The treatment of freed or runaway blacks presented a sticky dilemma for many Christian denominations in Indiana, which opposed slavery on religious grounds but considered colored people to be inferior creatures and not worthy of association with the white race. To reconcile this conflict, these church organizations and their followers endorsed colonization, with a view toward transporting Negroes to Africa. They further rationalized that blacks, not worthy of practicing Christianity in America, could spread the Good News to heathens in Africa. This movement was so strong that the Indiana Colonization Society was established in 1929.

Many states, like Indiana, used Jim Crow laws to deny people of color rights they were otherwise intended to receive under the 13th, 14th, and 15th Amendments to the U.S. Constitution, among them the unfettered right to vote and equal protection under the law, including free use of facilities open to the public and an equal education. In 1904, the Indiana Superintendent of Public Instruction, in his review of segregated public schools in Rockport, reported that black teachers earned $900 annually, compared to $1600 for their white counterparts. A single teacher taught all high school classes for Negro students. Unlike the curriculum for white students, there was emphasis on manual training and domestic science for colored youth.

In 1948, Democrat President Harry S. Truman undertook a crusade to pass federal civil rights legislation, including an anti-lynching law. The prevailing legislators, denying its passage, maintained that such laws were the province of the states, not the federal government, and, thus, unconstitutional. It was not until President Lyndon B.

Johnson, also a Democrat, championed the passage of the Civil Rights Act of 1964 that meaningful progress was made against unfair state laws that perpetuated discrimination on the basis of color. It was the first law to declare lynching to be a federal offense. This history changing enactment was followed by an equally monumental piece of legislation, the Voting Rights Act of 1965, which prohibited discrimination in voting. With the effort of Truman and the success of Johnson, black voters gradually left the Republican Party that had abolished slavery and started blacks on the road to freedom, and affiliated with the Democrats. As President Johnson had predicted, his party would lose the South; voters there gradually switched their party allegiance.

10 NEWSPAPER COVERAGE

Newspapers in communities along the Ohio River in
Indiana often expressed biased positions when it came to
race relations and the treatment of Negroes. On occasion,
the publications, espousing outright bigotry, appeared to be
marching hand in hand with the mob bent on carnage against
blacks. As noted by Pam Peters, author of *The Underground
Railroad In Floyd County*, the New Albany Daily Ledger, a
widely read newspaper, expressed such provocative language
in coverage of the shooting of two white men, Lansford and
Locke, by a black man, that the paper may have flamed the
fire of brutality during a 30 hour uprising of violence and
murder against Negroes. The Cannelton Telephone, on
December 20, 1900, described Rowland, Henderson, and
Rolla as "these cowardly devils, fiends incarnate and hell's

men...," further noting that the mob was too quick for the Indiana militia when it hanged the "coon," Joe Rolla. The following day, The English News, in referring to Rowland and Henderson as "two wretches richly deserv[ing] of death," printed this statement: "As a matter of fact, it would be strange if more of these brutal thugs, with whom every community seems to be more or less afflicted, should meet their fate at the hands of an enraged people." The following appeared in the Jeffersonville Evening News on December 27, 1900: "Too many privileges are given the blacks that they take advantage of that are entirely unnecessary...."

Other publications took a different perspective. The Boonville Standard, four days after Rolla's lynching, printed the following: "It is deeply regretted that Boonville and Warrick County should be disgraced by such violence." Alluding to the Thirteenth, Fourteenth, and Fifteenth Amendments, the Rockport Journal, on September 14, 1900, criticized the South and the Democrat Party:

> With the cry of "negro supremacy" on their lips, infuriated mobs have shot and driven the negro from the polls, have murdered him on the highway, have put him to death without the semblance of a trial, have destroyed his property, fired his

home and dealt him out torture and death as he fled the consuming flames.

The same paper described Captain Greathouse, ultimately acquitted of shooting Grandview's white Marshall, as industrious and trustworthy, whereas the rival newspaper, the Rockport Democrat, painted him to be a disorderly vagrant and further described the shooting of the officer as being intentional and not in self-defense. The Democrat's report may well have influenced the Rockport mob, leading its members to conclude that the failure to convict Greathouse was a miscarriage of justice not to be repeated with Rowland, Henderson, and Rolla.

11 SPENCER COUNTY BEFORE THE CIVIL WAR

Abraham Lincoln was born in Kentucky, a slave state, in 1809, when the nation's third president, Thomas Jefferson, was a slave holder. From age 7 to 21, Lincoln spent his formative years in Spencer County, Indiana, where Rockport was the county seat. Only a few blocks from where Rowland and Henderson were hanged by the mob, the future president, at age 19, left on a flatboat trip from Rockport's Lower Landing to New Orleans in 1828. There, witnessing slaves being sold on the auction block, he declared: "If I ever get a chance to hit that thing, I'll hit it hard."

With the promulgation of the Emancipation Proclamation and the Union's victory in the Civil War, he delivered on that promise. Spencer County was proud to have played an important role in his life, particularly in his education and his love of books.[5]

On January 28, 1838, in Springfield, Illinois, Lincoln, age 28, delivered what is known as the Lyceum Address, his reaction to the burning of a Negro by a mob in St. Louis a few weeks earlier. Addressing the threat to our hard-fought liberties, he declared:

> At what point is the approach of danger to be expected? I answer, if it ever reach us, it must spring up from amongst us. It cannot come from abroad. If destruction be our lot, we must ourselves be its author and finisher. As a nation of freemen, we must live through all time, or die by suicide. I hope I am over wary; but if I am not, there is, even now, something of an ill-omen among us. I mean the increasing disregard for the law which pervades the country; the growing disposition to substitute the wild and furious passions, in lieu of the sober judgment of the courts; and the worse than savage mobs, for the executive ministers of justice....

---

[5] *Abe's Youth, Shaping the Future President*, by William E. Bartelt and Joshua A. Claybourn, provides an excellent and thorough account of the positive influence of Spencer County and Souther Indiana on Abraham Lincoln, the man, during his formative years, age seven to 21.

Turn, then, to that horror-striking scene at St. Louis. A single victim was only sacrificed there. His story is very short; and is, perhaps, the most highly tragic, if anything of its length, that has ever been witnessed in real life. A mulatto man, by the name of McIntosh, was seized in the street, dragged to the suburbs of the city, chained to a tree, and actually burned to death; and all within a single hour from the time he had been a freeman, attending to his own business, and at peace with the world.

The question recurs, "how shall we fortify against it?" The answer is simple. Let every American, every lover of liberty, every well-wisher to his posterity, swear by the blood of the Revolution, never to violate in the least particular, the laws of the country; never to tolerate their violation by others.

The memory of Lincoln the man, their county's quasi-native son, and his defense of the rights and liberties of the people, was not in the minds of the vigilante horde in Rockport on December 16, 1900. They struck a blow to the heart of the country, advancing the commission of the suicide Lincoln feared.

Lincoln's plan for Reconstruction in the South following the Civil War emphasized reconciliation, not retribution. Unfortunately, the promise of black equality was rubbed in the faces of the Southern whites, leading to draconian measures to suppress those rights.

In ante-bellum times, Lincoln must have been aware of, and pleased with, the role of people in and around Rockport in the rescue of runaway slaves traveling by way of the Underground Railroad. There was a network of participation by its citizens.

In 1815, Levi Coffin, an abolitionist, founded the Underground Railroad in Indiana. Eventually, the clandestine course would spread across the north with routes originating in the slave holding south and stretching as far as British Columbia. Evansville, Rockport, New Albany, and Madison marked some of the main points of entry. Several thousand slaves escaped through Indiana, crossing the Ohio River to reach river towns or way stops near them.

A brief distance south of Rockport was a fisherman's shack on the Ohio River. Although the two occupants who lived there fished and sold their catch to passing steam boats, flat boats, and coal fleets, their chief business was secretly to ferry fugitive slaves across the river from Kentucky, house them, then pilot the Negroes to network friends who helped them reach the next station and eventually to freedom. Often, they were taken to the home of Ira Caswell where they were secured in the cellar or loft of his barn. Caswell fed them and gave them provisions for their next journey. The Rockport Inn, on Third and Walnut in Rockport, across from the courthouse, also served as a shelter for the refugees.

In face of the Fugitive Slave Act of 1850, which allowed slave owners or their agents to capture runaway slaves in non-slave holding states, and even enlist the aid of law enforcement, these protectors manning the Underground Railroad took great risks in hiding runaways and confronting the cruelty of the bounty hunters who tried to ensnare them.

Another connection point, just up river from Rockport, was in the charge of a book agent and peddler of fine stationery, Henry Johnson. He was assisted by a Negro named Ben Swain. The two men helped several slaves make their way on the Underground Railroad, eventually reaching destinations such as Canada and Liberia. Swain, who was elderly and a fugitive slave himself, had the opportunity to travel north and gain his freedom along with those he assisted. Swain declined the urgings that he seek his freedom. His response to those pleas was that he was getting old and wanted to help free members of his race while he still had time.

Swain's counterpart at Corydon, in Harrison County, was Oswald Wright, who helped numerous slaves escape across the Ohio River from Kentucky. For his involvement, he was arrested and imprisoned for five years at the state penitentiary in Frankfort, Kentucky's capital. His punishment, however, did not deter him from his mission to help fugitive slaves gain freedom. Once he had completed his term of incarceration, he returned to Corydon to resume his selfless role.

In Boonville, a group of abolitionists learned of the presence of men from Kentucky who were pro-slavery and who were bent on capturing free blacks, not slaves, and selling them to a slave trader located on the Ohio River near Owensboro. The Boonville contingent tracked down the Kentuckians and, with the threat of violence, drove them off. One Kentuckian lost an ear in the encounter when he vowed to carry out their mission.

Dr. John W. Posey of Petersburg, a leading anti-slavery champion, like Ira Caswell, acted as an important conduit in the course of the Railroad running from various stations, including Rockport. He and Caswell were instrumental in providing hiding places and in maintaining the path to freedom between their respective communities. Dr. Posey sheltered many runaway slaves in his coal shafts. During one close encounter, the two men, Posey and Caswell, along with several others assisting slaves along the Railroad route, were able to shield seven Negro fugitives from three Kentucky men and their bloodhounds out to capture the runaways and return them to their owners. In the course of the pursuit, three bloodhounds mysteriously died from poisoning.

The Willard Carpenter house in Evansville, which now houses WNIN Channel 9, an NPR station, was built in 1849 and is considered one of the finest examples of pure Georgian architecture. Owned by Willard Carpenter, a successful businessman and abolitionist, its location near the Ohio River made it one of the first stops for many runaway slaves. The historical marker in the front lawn reads: "Underground Railway Station. This is a site of an Underground Railway Station during the Civil War period. Runaway slaves were secretly hidden until they could be relayed to similar stations further north."

The role of Indiana's southern counties in sustaining the Underground Railroad marked contradictory times when compared to the air of white supremacy at the turn of the Twentieth Century.

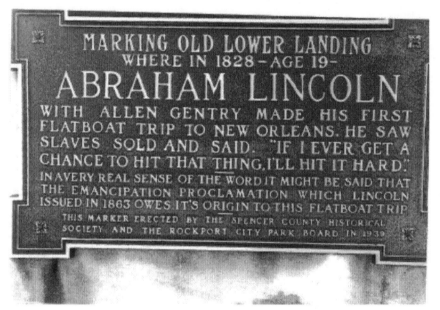

Abraham Lincoln monument commemorating his flatboat trip from Rockport to New Orleans, where, at age 19, upon witnessing slaves sold on auction, he declared his opposition to slavery.

Abraham Lincoln spent his formative years in Spencer County, Indiana, beginning at age seven and ending when his family moved to Illinois when he was 21. This sculpture sits in the rotunda of the Spencer County Courthouse in Rockport, the county seat, a community of about 2,000 people.

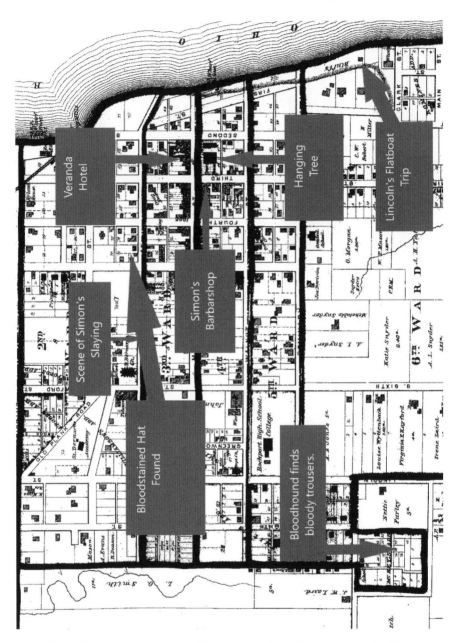

Plat of Rockport, a town with a population of approximately 2,800, showing places relevant to events described in the book.

EPILOGUE

A controversy has long raged over the origin of mankind. The wide consensus among genetic scientists holds that Homo sapiens, regardless of skin color, have a common, single origin, the continent of Africa. This "out of Africa" theory faces wide skepticism, primarily from the major religions, many of which maintain that mankind was created by a supreme being, and, for Judeo Christians, by and in the image of God.

If you accept the conclusions of molecular biologists, we are all related by a common ancestry. By the same token, if one believes in and follows the teachings and tenets of the dominant faiths, e.g., "do unto others...," there is no room for bigotry and discrimination, whether a person's skin is black, brown, white, red, yellow, or a variation thereof.

In a sense, we are all part of one race, the human race.

AUTHOR'S NOTE

The image on page 92 of this book is taken from an actual photograph of the men believed to be members of the mob that carried out the lynchings in the author's hometown of Rockport, Indiana, on December 16, 1900. The same image on the front cover was edited to omit the arrow pointing to the man standing prominently in the photograph, with the purpose of addressing the unedited photo separately in this note.

The original photo, along with entire front page of the Rockport Democrat, one of the newspapers that covered the event, came into the hands of my father, Harold Hargis, who was born in Cannelton, Indiana, in 1905, five years after the hangings. The newspaper article, dated December 21, 1900, had been passed down through his family on his mother's side. Her maiden name was Pfeifer, and the delivery name stamped on the newspaper was "Chris Pfeifer," an apparent relative of hers but not her father. Chris Pfeifer died in Rockport on February 23, 1900, several months before the work of the mob, so his widow may have entrusted the items to someone in the family.

The original photograph had been superimposed and glued in a position on the newspaper directly over the same image depicted in the photograph. My father had no information on the source of photo, the person who added the arrow, or any of the men shown, including the person at whom the arrow points. Hoping to find a name on the back, I removed the photo from its glued position, but no identity was found.

Unfortunately, the source of the arrow will remain a mystery. One can only assume that the marked subject played an important role in the malfeasance. His posture suggests a man proud and in control. Until my father showed me the newspaper article, I had no knowledge of the mob's lawless activities in Rockport and Boonville. This dark history needs to be told, in the same manner as the Equal Justice Initiative in Montgomery, Alabama, which memorializes hundreds of lynchings that occurred throughout the South.

The purpose of this publication is not to assign guilt for the transgressions of our former citizens but to gauge how far we have come and how far we, collectively and individually, need to go forward in normalizing race relations.

ACKNOWLEDGMENTS

My gratitude to my cousin, Jerriann Burroughs, for her literary and editing skills, to Cali Woodburn for her expertise in word processing, and to Ethan Miller, Brian Dawson, and Kirk Shelton and Katie Magill from Weir's Photo for their technical wizardry.

A special thanks to Amy Arnold Bellamy, author, who allowed me to reap the benefit of her bountiful creative writing skills and for her instructive guidance in self-publication and reaching an end product, and to Jane Ammeson, author, for her considerable input and for encouraging me to write this book of nonfiction.

A high salute and thanks to fellow author, Julia Walker.

A special note of appreciation to Betty Thomas and to my late cousin, Dorothy Hargis Kincaid, both high school English teachers, who instilled in me a love of English and a passion for writing.

A lifetime of gratitude to my late parents, H. L. "Gus" and Dorothy Hackleman Hargis, who ingrained in me the value and importance of learning, which was reinforced under the guidance of my elementary school teacher and principal, the late Truman May.

Most importantly, to my family, my wife, Connie, our daughter, Amy, and sons, Tom and Matt, my sisters, Ruth Ganchiff and Joan Hargis, and my brother-in-law, Jim Ballowe, all of whom have given me their loving support in writing this book.

BIBLIOGRAPHY

Rockport Democrat, July 6, 1900; October 5, 1900; December 21, 1900

Rockport Journal, March 24, 1899; July 6, 1900; September 14, 1900; October 5, 1900; December 21, 1900

Evening News (Jeffersonville, IN), December, 17, 18, 19, 21, 26, and 27, 1900

Pike County Democrat, December 16 and 21, 1900

The Republican (Corydon, IN), December 27, 1900

Corydon Democrat, December 26, 1900

Marshall County Independent, March 8, 1901

Indiana and the Ku Klux Klan, Indiana Center for History

The Ku Klux Klan in Indiana, Leonard J. Moore, University of North Carolina Press, 1997

Owensboro Daily Messenger, December 18 and 26, 1900

Owensboro Daily Inquirer, December, 17, 1900

Chicago Record, December 18, 1900

National Democrat (Jeffersonville, IN), December 21, 1900

Indianapolis Journal, December 18, 19, 21, 27, and 31 1900; February 2, 1901

Indianapolis News, December 17 and 18, 1900

Boonville Standard, December 21 and 28, 1900; January 4, 2001; February 8, 1901

Boonville Weekly Inquirer, December 21 and 28, 1900

Evansville Courier, December 17, 22, 23, 24, and 25, 1900

English News, December 21, 1900

Cannelton Telephone, December 20, 1900

Courier Bureau of Indianapolis, December 21, 1900

Lancing Michigan Sentinel, December 22, 1900

Washington D.C. Times, December 17, 1900

Belding Banner, Belding, MI, December 20, 1900

The Harrison County White Caps, A Project of the Historical Society of Harrison County, 2011

A History of Indiana from Its Exploration to 1922, Logan Esarey, 2009

Plat Book for Sunset Cemetery (Rockport, IN), p.57

Spencer County Criminal Order Book No. 3, pp. 208-9

History of the Underground Railroad, Col. William M. Cockrum, Heritage Books, 2005

The Negro In Indiana Before 1900, Emma Lou Thornbrough, Indiana University Press, 1993

Indiana in the Civil War Era, 1850-1880, Emma Lou Thornbrough, Indiana Historical Society, 1995

Indiana Blacks In the Twentieth Century, Emma Lou Thornbrough, Indiana University Press, 2000

Lyceum Address, Collected Works of Abraham Lincoln, 1953, Roy P. Basler, Editor

A History of Indiana from Its Exploration to 1922, Logan Esarey, 2009, Dayton Historical Publishing Company

Reminiscences of Levi Coffin, 1880, Cincinnati: Robert Clarke & Co.

Underground Railroad Sites: Fremont, 2009, Indiana Department of Natural Resourses

Burns Indiana Statutes, Indiana Code Section 3-8-1-20

Constitution of the State of Indiana, Article 6, Section 6

Chattanooga Daily News, January 29, 1901

The Underground Railroad in Floyd County, Pam Peters

Sundown Towns In The United States, James W. Loewen, 2005

Indiana's Sundown Ordinances, Donald M. Royer, 1965

Constitutional Law – Anti-lynching Legislation (1949), William Burnett Harvey

The Indianapolis Journal, December 31, 1900 and January 27, 1901

The Boonville Standard, February 8, 1901

Tell City Hews, December 29, 1900

Lincoln, Lynching, And A Long Way Home, Huffington
Post, January 10, 2018

Abraham Lincoln's Attitudes on Slavery and Race, Jorg Nagler,
American Studies Journal, 2009, Gottingen University Press

Boonville Inquirer, May 15, 1865

New Albany Daily Ledger, April 11, 1865

Evansville Journal, August 1, 3, 1865

"Modern Humans Came Out of Africa," National Geographic News,
July 18, 2007

Science Daily, University of Cambridge, May 10, 2007

Spencer County Census Records (1900 and 1910), Grandview, IN,
pp. 308-09, p.352

Spencer County Census Records (1880, 1900, 1910), Rockport, IN

Spencer County Death Records (1882-1920)

The Governors of Indiana, Linda C. Gugin, Indiana Historical
Society Press (2006)

Made in United States
Orlando, FL
25 March 2022

16138478R00067